Other Science I CAN READ Books

by MILLICENT E. SELSAM

PLENTY OF FISH

SEEDS AND MORE SEEDS

TONY'S BIRDS

A SCIENCE I CAN READ BOOK

TERRY
AND THE
CATERPILLARS

by
MILLICENT E. SELSAM

PICTURES BY ARNOLD LOBEL

HARPER & ROW
PUBLISHERS

To Terry Wolfson

—my indefatigable collector

of caterpillars and cocoons

Terry ran into the house.

"I have a caterpillar," she cried.

"Good," said her mother.

"What are you going to do with it?"

"Keep it," said Terry.

"Where?" said her mother.

"In a jar," said Terry.

Terry's mother gave her a jar.

Terry put the caterpillar in it.

She looked at the caterpillar.

How big and fat it was!

It was green.

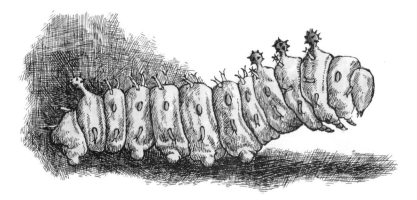

It had orange and yellow bumps on top.

It had blue bumps and spots on the side.

"This is the biggest, fattest, nicest

caterpillar I ever saw," said Terry.

The caterpillar started to move.

"This caterpillar will climb out,"
said Terry.

"Here is a top," said her mother.

Terry put the top on the jar.

"This caterpillar will get hungry,"
she said.

"What will I feed it?"

"Where did you find it?" said her mother.

"On the apple tree," said Terry.

"Then put some apple leaves in the jar,"
said her mother.

Terry picked some leaves
from the apple tree.

She put them in the jar.

Then she picked up the jar
and ran out of the house.

She saw her friend Benny.

"Benny," Terry cried,

"look at my caterpillar!"

"Ha," said Benny.

"Everyone knows you have to

make holes in the top.

How will the caterpillar live without air?"

Terry ran back into the house.

"Mother," she cried.

"How will my caterpillar

live without air?

Make some holes in the top, please.

Everyone knows you have to make

holes in the top."

"Everyone but me," said her mother.

And one by one she made

six holes in the top.

The next day Terry looked in the jar.

The leaves were almost gone.

"This caterpillar can eat!" she said.

"I'll get more leaves."

Every day Terry put more apple leaves

in the jar.

"I think," she said to her mother,

"this caterpillar is getting

bigger and fatter every day."

Terry wanted more caterpillars.

She looked for them

every time she went to pick leaves.

One day she found another

green caterpillar.

It had orange and yellow bumps on top.

It had blue bumps and spots on the side.

It looked the same as the first caterpillar.

The next day she found another caterpillar.

It looked the same, too.

Now Terry had three caterpillars.

She put each caterpillar in a jar.

Then she put little signs on the jars—

"Caterpillar 1," "Caterpillar 2,"

"Caterpillar 3."

Every day she took out all the dead leaves.

Then she cleaned the jars

and put in new apple leaves.

One morning Terry said to her mother,

"My first caterpillar

is not eating anymore.

"Maybe it had enough," said her mother.

Terry took the leaves out of the jar.

Then she saw that the caterpillar

was on a stick.

It was moving from side to side.

Silk was coming from its mouth.

"Funny," said Terry.

"I never saw that before."

Terry watched.

Swing, swing, bend, bend.

The caterpillar was moving all the time.

More and more silk came from its mouth.

Terry called her mother.

"Oh," said Terry's mother.

"Your caterpillar is making a cocoon!"

"Cocoon!" said Terry.

"What is a cocoon?"

"It is a silk house

a caterpillar makes for itself.

I have read about it, Terry, but I never

saw a caterpillar make a cocoon,"

said her mother.

"Why not?" asked Terry.

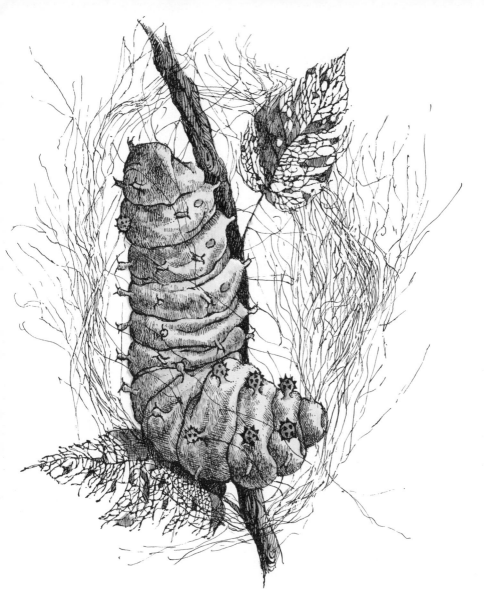

"Because I never picked up caterpillars
and kept them the way you do,"
said her mother.

It was time for Terry to go to school.

"I don't want to leave my caterpillar.

May I take it with me?" asked Terry.

"Of course," said her mother.

Terry took the jar to school.

"What do you have in that jar?"

asked her teacher.

"A caterpillar making a cocoon,"

said Terry.

"Really," said the teacher,

"that's something I never saw before."

"You, too!" said Terry.

"Maybe lots of us never saw it before,"

said the teacher.

She looked at the caterpillar.

Then, one by one, everyone in the class

looked at the caterpillar.

Benny was in the class.

"I saw this before,"

he said to the teacher.

"Good," she said.

"Now you can see it again."

"This caterpillar would not be

making a cocoon without those holes

in the top," Benny said to Terry.

"I know," said Terry.

"I bet you don't know

what happens next," said Benny.

"No," said Terry.

"What does happen next?"

"Find out," said Benny.

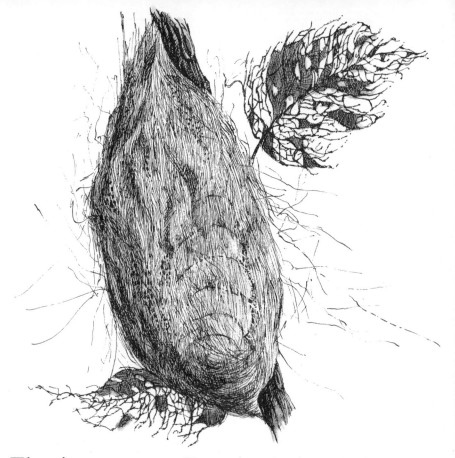

The jar was on Terry's desk all day.

Just before it was time to go home,

everyone had another look.

There was a thin silk tent

in the jar now.

Inside it the caterpillar was still moving.

26

That night Terry showed the cocoon

to her father.

"You can't see the caterpillar anymore.

But I think it is still moving inside.

I think it is making the inside walls

thicker and thicker."

"Maybe so," said her father.

"What happens next?" asked Terry.

"Nothing for a long time," he said.

But for Terry, lots of things happened.

One by one, each of her caterpillars

stopped eating.

One by one, each began to make

a silk cocoon.

Soon Terry had three cocoons.

"What shall we do now?"

she asked her mother.

"We will find out," said Terry's mother.

Terry and her mother went to the library.

When they came home,

they knew just what to do.

They found an old fish tank.

They put sand in the bottom of it.

Then, one by one, they put each cocoon

into the tank.

Then they covered the top of the tank.

"Now, Terry," said her mother,

"all you have to do

is wet the sand once a week.

That will keep the cocoons from

drying out."

"What will happen to them?" asked Terry.

"We shall wait and see," said her mother.

They put the tank in a cool place.

Terry wet the sand

every Monday before school.

If she forgot, her mother told her.

And so, all through the winter,

she wet the sand once a week.

One Monday in April

Terry went to put water in the tank.

A beautiful moth was sitting on a stick.

"Well," said Terry,

"I never put that in here."

31

She called her mother.

"Where did this come from?" she asked.

"Nothing could get into this tank.

This moth had to come

from something inside it."

"See if one of the cocoons

has a hole in it," said her mother.

Terry put her hand in the tank.

She picked up each cocoon.

"I think this one has a hole," she said.

She took the cocoon out of the tank.

"I can almost stick my little finger

through the hole," she said.

"This must be where that moth

came from."

"Did you know this would happen?"

she asked her mother.

"Yes, I knew," said her mother.

"But I never saw one come out before."

"Well, we didn't see this one

come out either.

But I know the moth came from

this cocoon," said Terry.

Terry sat still.

The moth sat still too.

She looked at the moth.

It was strange.

A caterpillar made the cocoon.

She had seen that with her own eyes.

But a caterpillar did not come out

of the cocoon.

A moth came out.

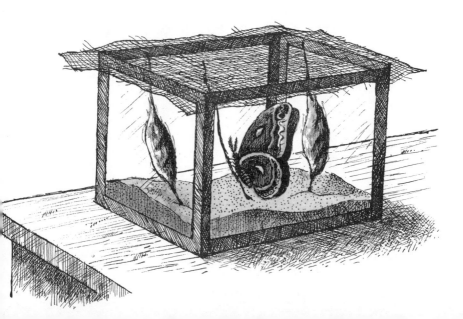

"I wonder," she said.

"I really wonder how this can happen."

"Things can change when they grow," said her mother.

"You change when you grow, too."

"But not this much," said Terry.

"If I changed this much when I grew, I would turn into a bird with wings."

"Well, it's just as well you can't," said her mother.

Terry had thought her caterpillars were

the most beautiful things in the world.

But the moth! It was even more beautiful.

It had big brown wings

with red and white edges.

There were four big white spots

on the wings.

Most of the day the moth was quiet.

But at night the big wings moved.

The moth flew a little inside the tank.

"Let's let it out," said Terry.

"All right," said her mother.

She took off the top of the tank.

Soon the big moth moved its wings

and flew up to a light.

The next day

Terry looked all over the room.

Where was the moth?

It was not on the light.

It was not on the floor.

She looked on the sofa and chairs.

The moth was gone.

Then she saw an open window.

"That's it," said Terry.

"That moth must be flying

around outside."

"Mother," Terry said,

"I want the other moths

to come out of their cocoons."

"They will come out

when they are ready,"

said her mother.

"I have to be ready, too," said Terry.

"This time I want to see one coming out."

"Well, we'll try," said her mother.

Four days went by

and nothing happened.

Terry's mother watched

when Terry was in school.

On Saturday Terry had to go

to a birthday party.

Terry's mother had to be

out of the house shopping.

Terry's father had to fix his car.

"I'll have to take the cocoons

to the party," said Terry.

"Fine," said her mother.

"Here's a plastic bag.

Carry them in this."

Terry put the cocoons in the bag.

45

When she got to the party,

she put the bag in back of her plate.

"Any minute a moth may come out,"

she told her friends.

"If it does,

we can sing Happy Birthday to it."

"Ha, ha," said Benny.

"Everyone knows moths only come out
of their cocoons at night!"

"Ha, ha!" said Terry.

"You think you know everything."

But that night Terry told

her mother and father what Benny had said.

"I'll call the museum on Monday,"

said her mother.

48

On Monday, Terry's mother called
the museum.

"Yes," said a voice on the telephone.

"Moths usually do come out
of their cocoons at night."

"Well," said Terry's mother,

"we will have to work this out.

Terry, you can look at the cocoons
before you go to bed.

I'll watch till I go to bed.

Daddy will get up once in the night
to look.

You will look again
in the morning, Terry."

Tuesday, Wednesday,

and Thursday went by.

Nothing happened.

On Friday night Terry said, "I think

I will kiss my cocoons goodnight."

She bent down to kiss the cocoons.

Her head came up fast.

"I hear a noise," she said.

"Maybe something is going to happen

at last," said her father.

"We will call you if it does, Terry,"

said her mother.

Later Terry's mother heard noises

in one of the cocoons too.

"Well," she said to Terry's father,

"Be sure to have a good look tonight."

"I will," he said.

At four in the morning

Terry's father got up

to look at the cocoons.

"At last," he cried, "something

is happening."

A little body was pushing its way out

of one of the cocoons.

Terry's father ran to get his wife.

Then they went to Terry's bed.

"She is so fast asleep," he said.

"But she has waited so long.

Wake her up," said Terry's mother.

Then the three of them went

to look at the cocoons.

"It's almost out," cried Terry.

Slowly the moth pulled itself

out of the cocoon.

It looked wet and soft.

"Its wings look so tiny," said Terry.

"Wait," said her father.

Soon Terry said, "I think the wings

are getting bigger. Are they growing?"

"Not really," said her father.

"The moth is pumping them up

with blood."

It took a long time.

But slowly the moth's wings

got bigger and bigger.

And the moth's body

got smaller and smaller.

At seven o'clock, Terry said,

"How big its wings are!

It looks like the first moth now."

"Let's go back to bed,"

said Terry's mother.

"It's Saturday. We can sleep late."

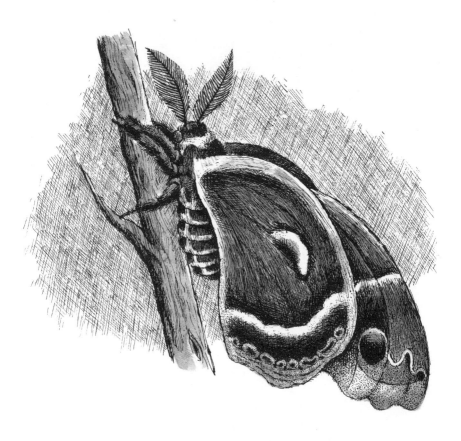

When Terry woke up,

she went to the tank.

"I want to keep this moth

for a few days," she said.

"Then I'll give it some more room

in the tank," her father said.

He made a high roof over the tank.

No one got up Saturday night.

But on Sunday morning another moth

was sitting in the tank.

"My goodness," said Terry.

"The other one is out."

For a few days the two moths

flew around the tank.

The two moths

did not look quite the same.

Terry saw the difference.

One had a bigger, fatter body.

"That's the female, or mother moth,"

said her father.

"She is full of eggs."

The other moth had bigger feelers

in front of its head.

"That's the male," said Terry's father.

"Is he the father moth?" asked Terry.

"Yes," said her father.

The next day Terry saw

something strange.

The mother moth was leaving

little round things on the stick.

Terry called her father.

"What are those?" Terry asked.

"Those are the eggs

coming out of the mother moth.

I told you she was full of eggs."

"What will come from them?" she asked.

"Caterpillars," said her father.

"More caterpillars!" cried Terry.

"You mean we can make
our own caterpillars?"
"We can't make them, Terry,
but the moths can," said her father.

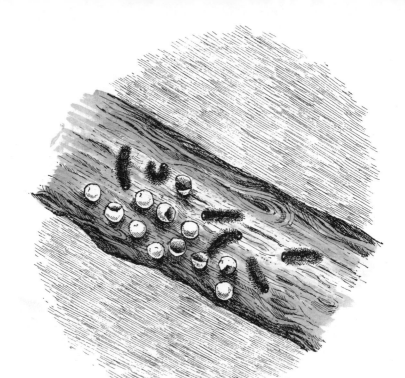

"So far I see only eggs," said Terry.

But ten days later Terry saw

little caterpillars come out of the eggs.

"Oh, they are black," said Terry.

"They are supposed to be green."

"They change color as they grow,"

said Terry's mother.

"They will look like

your other caterpillars

when they get big."

"I'll put these back on the apple tree,"

said Terry.

"I know what is going to happen.

The caterpillars will get bigger and bigger.

Then they will make cocoons.

Next year the mother and father moths

will come out of the cocoons.

And then the mother moth will lay eggs.

Caterpillars will come out of the eggs.

And then the whole thing will start again."